OTHER WORKS BY THIS AUTHOR

You Bet Your Life After Death

The 5th Secret

The 4 Secrets of the Universe

All About the Soul's Journey

The Book of Manifesting

Mysteries, Prophecies, and the Hollow Earth

The Lightness of Being

Sojourn

Poet Gone Wild

Poems of Life, Love, and the Meaning of Meaning

Infinite Healing

Poems and Messages for the Loss of a Loved One

Poems and Messages for the Loss of Your Animal Companion

The Moment of Death

An Awakening into Awareness, Healing, and Love

PAUL GORMAN

Copyright © 2025 Paul J. Gorman
All Rights Reserved

Year of the Book
135 Glen Avenue
Glen Rock, PA 17327

ISBN 13: 978-1-64649-516-0 (print)
ISBN 13: 978-1-64649-517-7 (ebook)

Cover and interior photos licensed from Alamy, unless otherwise noted.

No part of this publication may be reproduced, distributed, or transmitted in any form or by any means, including photocopying, recording, or other electronic or mechanical methods, without the prior written permission of the author, except in the case of brief quotations embodied in critical reviews and certain other noncommercial uses permitted by copyright law.

Library of Congress Control Number: 2025920468

Disclaimer:
This book contains spiritual messages and information, channeled from people who have died.

Some names of people I knew have been altered for privacy.

Contents

Foreword 1
Introduction 3
My Life as a Bumble Bee 4

Part I
Cleopatra 9
Frank Sinatra 13
Elvis Presley 15
Anne Frank 17
John F. Kennedy 19
Mother Teresa 21
Cleopatra (again) 23
Judy Garland 26
Robin Williams 29
Rosa Parks 32
Abraham Lincoln 34
Tyrone Power 37
Rod Serling 40
George Carlin 43
Dad 46
George Washington 48
Edgar Cayce 51
Bob Hope 54
George Burns 58
Jimmy Stewart 63
Leslie Nielsen 66

Part II
Hillen 71

Pete 73
Jackie 75
Dave & Russell 77
Wayne 79
Buck 81
Marty 83
Lynda 85
Rich 87
Loriann 89
Loriann (again) 91

Part III
John Candy 95
Bob Newhart 97
Freddie Mercury 98
David Bowie 100
George Harrison 102
John Lennon 103
Dr. Martin Luther King, Jr. 104
Wolfgang Mozart 106
Vincent Van Gogh 108
BJ 109
Baron B. 111
Dave C. 112
Paul P. 113
Colin M. 114
Doc 115
Mack 116
Andrew & Jay 117
A Soul Director 119
Leroy 120
John S. 121

Chris T. 122
Marty (again) 124

Part IV
More Time, Or Not 129
Angel Death 131
The 5 Shapes of Death 132
A Guardian Angel 135
A Person's Spirit 137
Afterword, Cleopatra 139
Affirmations 141
About the Author 142

Foreword

This book is about the moment of death—communicated to me from spirits of those who have died.

You will recognize some of the names of well-known historical figures and personalities; others are people that I knew in life.

Their accounts of the death moment are fascinating, and they all have a common theme—that it is an awakening into all awareness healing, and love.

For us still living, it is more like the moment we transitioned into all shock, loss, and grief.

This book will give you perspectives from 'the other side'—the soul perspectives of *The Moment of Death: An Awakening into Awareness, Healing, and Love.*

Introduction

I was trying to describe the moment of death to my friend Alex—at least my understanding from what spirits had communicated to me—and I couldn't explain it very well. How could I?

That inspired me to make this book, with a compilation of the descriptions that spirits had related to me.

It is arranged into 3 parts:

Part 1 is 21 new chapters of messages from famous historical figures.

Part 2 is 22 excerpts of the death moment descriptions, from messages that are in my book, *The 5th Secret: In the Universe that I Am*.

Part 3 is 11 excerpts from *All About the Soul's Journey: Understanding Death*—messages from people I had known, who have died.

Also included are the chapters 'More Time, or Not' and 'Angel Death' from *The 5th Secret*, and from *The 4 Secrets of the Universe*, the chapters 'The 5 Stages of Death', 'A Guardian Angel', and 'A Person's Spirit'.

My intention is for these accounts to give readers a clearer insight into the death moment.

I have learned that we are given choices, and when we do decide to leave the Earth, it is an exhilarating departure from an illogical planet of both love and non-love—where the love is God.

The non-love experience will be over. What did we learn from it? What is the purpose of our being in it?

The following message was written after all of the other chapters, and it gives us a snapshot of life, purpose, healing, gratitude, death, and God—coming from a bee.

My Life as a Bumble Bee

A few weeks ago, I rescued a bumble bee that was floating face-down in a dish of water outside.
I thought it may have drowned, but when I gently poured out the water in the grass, it crawled away and went under the deck. Can I speak with the bee?

I am a bee having been rescued by you in an instance of allowing me another chance to live.

All I can give in exchange for my life is a healing in your mind that has no limitations—meaning it is eternal in width, infinite in length, and unlimited in depth. It has nothing but God in it.

Call on me, and I can become the pollinator of your dreams.

I read that worker bees only live for a few weeks, so you may be gone now, but did you do okay after I got you out of the water?
I lived about 8 more days in my life as a bee, and I had a lot of work that I got done. It is never done, because it is an eternal process, but I did my part for all of the plants to have their pollination.

Thank you for your job well done, and for your healing gift.
I am incredibly grateful for having met you in my healing of the Earth.

Can you please tell me what it was like the moment you died?
All I had in my mind became what is known as a light having no attributes besides God—or all I could be, having nothing but love for myself.

PART I

Cleopatra

Can I speak with Cleopatra?
I am Cleopatra. How may I help you?

I am making a book about the death moment. Can you please tell me what the experience was like for you?
I can, but it was a long time ago, in your timeline.

Your name is still very famous.
I cannot be more elated than hearing that.

Why so? My understanding is that peoples' minds heal when they die, and they lose all of their earthly concerns.
I can enjoy hearing it from you though.

Have you heard it from others, or checked in on the Earth?
I have—but it made me a little bit elated—not a lot.

Why does my comment make you so elated?
Because I am having a Gorman communication. You are well known here in the spirit world.

I am doubtful, and am little-known here in the physical world... just sayin'.
I can assure you, I am not exaggerating.

This book is a compilation of excerpts of what spirits have told me that each of their death experiences was like. Yours will be the first chapter in the book.

I am so elated again! I know you think it will not be read by many people, but I can help illuminate it in all peoples' minds that need to heal from reading it.

Thank you, Cleopatra. I am ready for your account.

I died in my early 40s, in my life as Cleopatra.

All I can hear in your mind is that records say I was 39. I was in my early 40s at the time of my death.

Adding hatefulness to my death is not a very happy subject, but I was forced into ending my life by men who had more power than I had.

I am sorry about that. This is a rough planet, but I expect for the wickedness to be gone soon, and for a new era of purification to begin.

I can give you all the highlights if you want, but it can be for another Gorman communication.

That would be great, and I'd like to know more about your life. Let's start with your life ending. Did you feel ecstasy?

All I felt had healed me so completely, that I couldn't have felt better.

Having lived and died is all I needed for my healing to be complete. I became a light being, if you could imagine it.

After I died, an angel came into my awareness, and asked if I could imagine I was not in my life anymore. I answered in the affirmative, and my head exploded in light—but it also felt very good.

After that, we motioned away from the Earth.

Thank you, Cleopatra. That is all very interesting. I would like to discuss more topics in my future, assuming I have one.
I can heal it in your mind, so there is the future you desire.

Thank you for that. We will talk about it then.
I am at home in your mind. Can I remain here for a while?

For how long? Do you just want to observe the Earth through me?
I am energizing your mind, and I will be leaving before one week has passed.

Okay, I will guide you, and you can guide me.
I am elated again. How can I thank you?

You may not be thanking me in a week—you may be begging to get away :)
I can enjoy all of your lighthearted humor in my despair.

I will be communicating with others to complete this book, so it will be like a Zoom call where you are muted at those times.
I understand, and will be listening only.

Can you give me a title for this book?
The Moment of Death: An Awakening into Awareness, Healing, and Love.

I like it—the title, I mean. Death, not so much...
It is not as awful as it appears. How awful could it be to become one in God?

You will have to find out, and I will greet you when you arrive.

That would be awesome... the greeting part.
I am hearing what is in your mind. Did we know each other in another timeline? Yes, in one timeline, I had actually been in your family. We were distant cousins, but had never met each other. We knew about each other.

This will be a great first chapter, giving readers an overview of my conversations.
I am going to be silent now, for our communication to resume in another agreed upon session.

Frank Sinatra

Can I speak with Frank Sinatra?
Hello, Gorman. I am already hearing what is on your mind. I can hear it, and I can also heal it.
I am in a Light Body now, having no earthly attachments anymore.
I can allow myself an instance of healing in your mind, if it is allowed by you.
I know all of your questions, before you are about to write them.
How could I have died, and not been included in your last book?
I don't have an answer for that, but I know how you enjoyed my music.
All I can hear is, what was it like when I died? I had it coming, but don't we all?
I had it coming because I didn't believe it would be so wonderful, at least for me.
I thought it might be all over, but it was not all over—it was just beginning, meaning my understanding and awareness.
God has a plan, and it is your plan—because God and you are one.
You and I are also one, meaning God is everyone and everything that has love of life in it.
What happened when I died, you are asking? I had an uneventful heart attack, because my heart couldn't pump anymore. At that moment, I died.

Lightness enveloped me, and I got pulled into it from the top of my head.
I felt like I had never felt before. I had experienced bliss—a bliss I cannot explain with words.
Lightness, God, or whatever it can be called, is what it was.
After that, my guardian angel asked me if I was alright. "All I am is all, as in alright" is what I had said, and it acknowledged my answering cleverly, and we headed away from the Earth at that point.

Thank you, Frank. That is all I needed for now. This is a book about the moment of death experience. Yours was very interesting!
I had it coming, like I said. We all have it coming to us—to heal ourselves back into Oneness.

Your grave marker says, "The Best is Yet to Come"—the title of one of your songs.
It is all I can leave on the Earth, with my music.

Elvis Presley

May I speak with Elvis Presley?
I am here, and I can answer your questions about my death in particular, and death in general. It is all I had hoped for in my Christian faith.
All Christian faith means is believing in God, or believing in nothing but yourself—meaning in "The King," which is yourself. God is the king, and you are God.
It cannot be any other way in heaven.

Thank you, Elvis. Can you please tell me what it was like for you when you died?
I had one or two too many pills and they interacted with my heart, making it stop its pumping blood. How could I have been on so much medication?—is what I usually hear.
I liked my life, but I didn't like myself enough to love myself. Loving oneself is all you really need to do, because all are one.
Loving one is loving God, which is love—making non-love an impossibility.
How could love not love itself if it is love? It cannot.
Love is all there can ever be, meaning love is all there is—and all is God then.
I am God, and you are God. We just didn't have the awareness to understand it on the Earth.
It is all we need to know though.

What was your death experience like?
I had been taking pills before having a nap. In my nap dreaming, I met an angel named "Eld."
I thought, "Eld and Elvis—how's that for a combination of names?"
Eld asked me if I had been expecting an angel today. I said I did not expect an angel, and it gave me an insight that I had not considered. I did expect an angel—it was my last day on Earth.
After I realized it was my time to leave, a light in my head had illuminated as intensely as you can imagine. Into the light I went, and we headed away from the Earth.

Did you collapse in the bathroom?
I had gotten into the bathroom in my half-asleep mode, yes.

Thank you, Elvis.
I thank you for giving me this opportunity to speak.

Anne Frank

May I speak with Anne Frank, who died in 1945, at age 15?
Anne Frank allows herself a Gorman communication.
I can communicate with Gorman.
All I can hear is if I am alright now. I am all, and all can only be alright.
How could I help you if I was not "all right"? All I can hear is if I can describe how my death healed me.
I can, and all deaths are healing. Mine allowed me an only escape from a prison camp in Germany, during the Second World War. My life had been a hell on Earth, if there is a hell—always hiding for a long time, and then to be arrested and imprisoned. It became a lot worse from there, and death had been an event that was welcomed, and it also was healing. It was not what I expected. I expected to have more evil in my experience, and to suffer more.
All I could feel was exhilaration, and ecstatic escape in my being dead.

Thank you, Anne. Did you die from typhus?
I died from a broken heart, and was defeated by typhus in my last moments, yes.
I am hearing if I was greeted by an angel in my death. I could have—I did not pay attention in my new elated awareness.
I am hearing if I have more to communicate to you. All I can describe is how much I disliked my last few

years of life. How could a little girl have found herself in the mouth of evil, I hear in your mind?
It is the human antithesis of love to be hateful. How can humans be so hateful?
They believe in having an evil enemy, and it is how controllers can manipulate them to do anything.
How can it not be an obvious deception?
If it can be believed, it can be accepted. If it is accepted, it cannot be a deception any longer.

Thank you, Anne.

Anne Frank has this I can add to your communication. Allow God into your life, and ask God to block all deception from being allowed into your mind.
Ask God to block it, and God answers in the affirmative, always.

In your culture, I can acknowledge there is little truthfulness.

John F. Kennedy

Can I speak with President John F. Kennedy?
I had always been called Jack, if it is okay with you.

You were admired by everyone—except for a few creatures who didn't like the truth being spoken.
I had an indescribably good life, until I was shot. I had only been honest in my appearances though.
How can I help you? I can hear that I am asked about my death.
I did not expect it in that moment, but I had expected I would not live a long life. How could I live a long life if I was not honest with myself?

Please tell me about your death.
I had not been expecting it, but it came at the right moment.

Why was it the right moment?
I could have been injured, or delayed my death, but an angel had given me guidance in the moments after being shot. It said I could go back a few seconds, and carry on without being shot.
I did not think it was best to continue my life.

Why not?
It had been decided before I entered into my life that it would not be as long as it could have been.
I chose it, and could have changed it, but did not. I can describe it for you, if you would like me to.

First, was your death in November 1963 necessary for the country, and the world?
In a dream having a healing objective, it had a lot to heal in its horror, and in its dealing a fatal blow to an admired leader.

Did you feel any pain?
I felt an explosion of light all around me in the moment I was hit with gunfire that hit my head.
An angel appeared in my head, and was giving me guidance on how I could proceed.
I could go away from the Earth with it, or I could go back a few moments and continue my life, until another time when it would be over.

Did you see the motorcade continue on?
I could hear everything, and also witness it from my advanced awareness.

Thank you, Jack. The world wanted you to stay. Would you like to add anything else?
In a dream of light and dark, be the light.

Mother Teresa

May I speak with Mother Teresa?
I can allow myself to acclimate to your mind, yes.

I would like to get your comments from your advanced awareness, and learn about your death experience.
I am all healing light now. Before I died, I was not completely illuminating.
I could have been all healing light in my life, but I had a big ego that defended my position on worldly affairs.
It made me incapacitated in my healing ability.

Can you please tell me what you experienced when you died in 1997?
I had heart failure because I could not have love for a lot that was in my mind.
In the moment when my heart had its last beat, a lot of angels came into my awareness, and asked me if I could imagine going with them to meet God.
I acknowledged in the affirmative, and my head exploded in light—meaning, I became God in that moment of all lightness, and all peacefulness.

What happened after that?
I could not have been more illuminated since that moment, although all moments are an instant in God.

Did you become one with God then—meaning, did you not proceed to move away from the Earth, and have a Lifetime Review, etc,?
I did not have a Lifetime Review, although I have always had instances of introspection.

Thank you, Mother Teresa. Can people call on you for healing light?
I can heal those in need of an intercession if called upon, yes.

Cleopatra (again)

[Later in the week]

Cleopatra, are you still with me?
I am Cleopatra, and I am inside your mind, yes.

Sorry that you picked kind of a down week for me.
I can guide in my limited capacity as a spirit. All humans are allowed to be and do as they please, even if all have hostile egos, and intentions having little goodness or honesty.
All I can feel is dismay and disappointment in your encounters with others.
My admonition is to not let it bring you down. In a dream, there can only be one point of reference in its illumination, and it is you. Others can be illuminating in your dream, but not projecting it.
Allow everyone else to illuminate their weaknesses in your dream, then they can't possibly be harmful to you.

How about if they illuminate a little kindness, love, and gratitude or appreciation?
It has a lifetime of opportunity that is always presented, but not always illuminated in human minds.
Affirming a mantra has a lot of power—"I allow all of the other people in my dream to be all I am not willing

to be—unhealed egos in self-hating egoland, not having any gratitude or love for its ego demands."

That's really good. What can I do to keep my mind positive, peaceful, healed, and manifesting my desires?
Ask it one thing every time it feels a disappointment—"Would I rather be him or her? I don't have that kind of punishment in mind."

That's great!
I am elated that I can help the one who is so well known here!

That's what I wanted to ask you. How, or why am I well-known in the spirit world?
All I am allowed to tell you is you will be the next big spiritualist writer in your lifetime.

I don't really believe it, but will try to keep my books interesting and informative.
It has been deemed important on the Earth for your books to be widely disseminated.

I like writing the books, and also making the covers.
All have the most impressive covers, but even more impressive is each one's content between the covers.

Thank you, Cleopatra—you know you can stay on as long as you like.
I know, it had been a thought I heard in your mind.

I am going to get your 2 mantras printed on a card—one mantra on each side. I can look at it

every time I go up the street and see the neighbor that snarls at me. I call her "Hoss."
Allowing a little bit of laughter can make a bad dream into a lighthearted comedy.

I think only 2 or 3 people have read *The 5th Secret*, which was published a few weeks ago. I am about to publish *You Bet Your Life After Death* in the next month, immediately followed by this book.
All will become more widely read after the next two.

My thought is that those will be easier for me to promote—because of the humor in one, and the insights in the other.
Allowing humor and insights to heal in the minds of all who read them.

Judy Garland

Can I speak with Judy Garland?
I am delighted I can be heard by Gorman in his mind.

Hello, Judy. I am writing a book about the moment of death. Can you please tell me what your experience was like?
I am sorry that you died at the young age of 47, and I really enjoyed your singing—especially in *The Wizard of Oz* movie.
I died from having too many anti-depressants in one night. What I needed had nothing to do with taking pills.
I needed a lot of love, and it had to come from inside of me, having no other place it could come from.

Did you know you had died at first?
I knew, and it didn't matter in my logic. I lived in the limelight, and would have traded it for love any day.

Did angels meet you?
I had been met in my mind by angels, and also a guide advisor who had always been with me.
He—if he had a gender—helped me throughout my life.
"Am I really dead?" is what I said to them, and they all said it was my choice if I wanted it.

I imagine it was like when you were Dorothy in *The Wizard of Oz*. The Good Witch Glenda said

all you have to do is click your heels together 3 times, and say, "There's no place like home."
I had not considered it like that, but it was a lot like that scene.

Please tell me about your experience.
A guide, and my angels—of which there were four—all came into my head like it was a meeting about how I could live or die in the next moment, if I chose that option. Needless to say, I had decided I did not want to live any longer.
I was in a delightful, blissful world of lightness and lovingness.
As soon as I made my decision known, I had the most intense light in my head that pulled me into it all the way, from my head.

Then what happened?
I had died at that moment, and it was exhilarating, to say the least. I was God in that moment- all lovingness, and all peacefulness.
"In that moment" is in all moments, because all in God is one instant.

Thank you, Judy. Would you like to add anything else?
I illuminate in love now. Be love, and illuminate God in life.

Robin Williams

Can I speak with Robin Williams please?
All rise for Robin Williams, the one having risen from the dead!

Funny.
I had to make it funny, or it couldn't be believed I am Robin Williams.

Do you know why I asked to speak with you?
Because I am dead, and it makes deadness an interesting conversation piece—not my deadness, just deadness in general—unless it's a dead audience, and then deadness might have some meaning, but they might like to hear about aliveness then.
I can hear—it is "deadness" on your mind. How could I have known that?
I am a lot more alive now than in my dead-end life—that I could not heal, without making myself dead, I mean. I cannot die now because I am dead, so I have nothing to worry about.
Actually, I was God in a Robin Williams costume, and had no idea until I became all I could be in dying.
How could I be all I could have been without dying? It is easier than dying—I can tell you that much.
Dying is always messy—intentional or not, it leaves a discarded body for others to declare dead, and then either prepare it for burial, or dispose of it in a funeral pyre that has more of an oven look and feel to it.

There should be other options like feeding the dead body to alligators, or allowing it an instantaneous evaporation in a bizarre cult-like incineration in a personal-sized atomic reactor that could light up a city for a few days.

Poof! That would be my preference, if the alligators didn't eat everything first.

It is the "No-mess Death Option" marked on your driver's license. It cannot be changed, unless it is changed for you by another person who doesn't want you leaving a mess.

Haa, haa!

I can help in your no-mess death inquiries without making a mess, I promise.

Were you met by angels when you died? I understand that you had hanged yourself in 2014, at age 63.

I did hang myself, making me a heavier mess to take down and prepare for a proper death—not the alligator dinner option, but another of the options I had not checked on my license.

Okay, I am going to ask you 'Yes or No' questions. Did angels give you an option to go back into your dead-end life at the moment you died?

I had it as an option, so yes—but I declined by saying "No," so it is yes then no.

Did you feel all lovingness and peacefulness, with no desire to go back into an unhealed body?

I had no desire to go back into my hanging body, as I would have had a hard time explaining the rope around my neck.

Could you have gone back further in time to before you decided to put a rope around your neck?
I could have, but the alligator park was closed.

Can you be serious for a minute? I know the answer is "No."
I was going to say it for you, but heard "No," and will stick with that. If I said "Yes, I could be serious for a minute," then I would only be serious at being comical.

Thank you, Robin. People will be happy to read your comical responses... the handful of people who may read this.
I only allowed myself to be comical because I illuminated in a comedy and a tragedy, having mostly messy endings.

Rosa Parks

May I speak with Rosa Parks, who died of natural causes in 2005, at the age of 92?
I heard my name called, and I am in your mind, in your timeline.

You were an important figure in my timeline, known for your courage in refusing to obey laws that were unfair—and are now illegal. Your simple refusal to move to the back of a bus was a pivotal moment in civil rights history, in the United States.
I could have moved, but I didn't have any desire to give into a growing hatefulness on a public bus, so I decided not to move, despite my hateful onlookers.

You are considered a hero—one who risked physical harm and imprisonment for defying injustice.
I am not a hero—I was a human being defying a lie that I was inferior in life.
God was in the courage, and evil was in the lie.

Despite health challenges, you went on to live a long life. Can you please tell me what your moment of death was like? It is for a book.
I had an especially peaceful death in my old age. In my bedroom, I was met by angels on numerous occasions, and I also had some visitations by my relatives from their home in God.

After my last visit, an angel asked me if I was ready to be in God also. I said I was, and in my head I had an incredible bright light illuminating and pulling me into it, head-first.

I had imagined it could be like that, but it was far better than I imagined. I had died, but I also had come alive at that moment. I would describe it as being in an electrifying atmosphere of love, and having no earthly desires or needs anymore.

God has illumination for everyone. It can be asked for, and it is always given.

Thank you very much, Rosa!
I can add another aspect of God for your book.
All God is, is all God can even be in a human—it is love, and having the courage in life to defy any non-loving actions, thoughts, words, and decrees like the one I defied.

Abraham Lincoln

With whom can I speak next about the moment of death?
Abraham Lincoln asks if he can be heard in your mind, and if he can be included in the Gorman communications.

Abraham Lincoln's name popped into my head twice today, when I was considering the next chapters.
Abraham has a lot he can tell you about the moment of death. Abraham Lincoln here. I heard that I am going to be included in your next book.

Word gets around. Who told you that? It was just decided.
I am God, alternating as an individual soul named Abraham Lincoln—so I heard it from the first time you thought of it.

Hello, Mr. Lincoln. You were an admired leader. Where I am now happens to be not far from Gettysburg, and the battlefield where you gave your now-famous speech.
I always have my Civil War instance of death to heal in my soul.

What do you mean?
I was allowed a number of death moments in my last year, and in my death on April 15th of that year, I was

instrumental in ending the Civil War's incredible bloodshed and number of casualties.

General Lee surrendered the week before you were killed, and the war was formally ended months later.
I could have had another death moment in my last year, but I decided I could leave after General Lee's surrender.

Why?
My Lifetime Agreement had been to halt the bloodshed in a horrific civil war that could have lasted a lot longer.

What was it like when you died?
I died in an illumination of light having no comparison. All I could hear was a lot of commotion after being hit in my head.
In hindsight, I know I had been hit by a gunshot. Although I had life in my body, I died in the moment I had been hit in the head.
Angels came into my head and had informed me I had died. I asked if I could leave, and immediately I came into a large theater like the one I had been killed in. It was a performance of my life, and I could be in it again, playing the part of others I had met in my lifetime on the Earth.

Thank you, President Lincoln.
I can give instructions on how I would have conducted my life differently. In hindsight again, I made a lot of enemies in my life because I did not have their interests in my heart, along with my own.

Having both interests in my heart heals them in an illumination of forthrightness and generosity, making them merged.

Thank you, Mr. Lincoln.
I am obliged, Mr. Gorman.

Tyrone Power

Who can I speak with next?
I heard my name—I am Tyrone Power.

Your name popped into my head.
I heard it in that exact moment also. It was a God insight. I am hearing in your mind how I died of a massive heart attack. I had not heeded doctors' advice about not exerting myself.
Anyway, I had died, and could have avoided it even after I died.

Did you choose to leave when you did?
I had had enough of life in my Hollywood lifestyle of non-committal romances, as I had been a contributor to them.

What was it like when you died?
I died in an ambulance, and I could hear it, and see it from the outside. I exited my body when my heart had stopped. I had a heart of gold, but gold gets itself into a lot of battles on the Earth that it does not need to be in, or need to win. My gold heart finally broke.

I know what you mean.
I could have lived a lot longer if I did not put my heart into it, though.

Did you have intense illumination in your head when you died?

I had it in the moment I fell down from the heart attack, yes. I lived a little while longer, and observed myself being transported in an ambulance to a hospital.

Then what?
Angels came into my head and asked me if I had any questions about what had just happened.
I said I had one—"If I could have lived my life a lot happier, how could I have done it?"
The answer had many insights for me, and it was a question they answered me with—"How could I have loved myself in life, more than I did?" I allowed myself indulgences and addictions that were not healthy for me.
I can only indulge in healing myself with the help of God now.

Thank you, Tyrone.
I can give another helpful anecdote, if it will help all who will be reading this.
Being dead is a lot like being alive—except in death, all that has meaning for you is God's love and healing.
It is available in life, and why you were born—to heal in looking for it inside yourself.

Those are beautiful words of wisdom. Thank you, Tyrone.
I am healing in your asking me why I had died, so I am thanking you. I had not fully appreciated my actions, even though I was an actor.

Rod Serling

I think I will now be speaking with Rod Serling.
Imagine if you can, in a world of no time or space, having only God.
How could it be healed, and have human minds in it?
It can only be in a twilight zone of imagination, where every thought becomes a force in it.
I am the host now, for the rest of your life—in The Twilight Zone.

You did not disappoint, Rod! I could even hear creepy music during your monologue, with a screech at the end.
I can help in your dream interpretation, because that is what you are doing.
You are in a dream, and having a dream that doesn't make sense.
In God's universe, there is no separation—but you allow it as a reason to escape from the dream.
It can be enjoyed, or it can be endured—it is your choice.
I enjoyed my dream, and left it promptly after my work was done.
All I could hear in my heart attack was, "Here he comes!"
I heard it, and knew right away how I could exit the dream.
Then I came back into my body, and heard "There he goes back into his body."

I thought about hearing both of those statements for 2 days, then left again—but for good the second time, having no reason to remain on the Earth.

Can you tell me how you felt when you died?
I felt all lovingness and peacefulness—and expansiveness that I cannot begin describing.
How I could begin describing it is like holding your breath underwater for a full minute—which is your life—then having burst up and out of the water into incredible lightness, with nothing holding you back.
I had illustrated a lot of its mysteries in my television writing.

You did, and your work still remains some of the finest work done in supernatural dramas.
I enjoyed having a lot of hardworking and talented people helping me, because I came into life to create the episodes, in the new medium of television.

Do you have a favorite theme, looking back?
I had always been fascinated by time being flexible, or non-linear. It does not even exist, except in every person's dreaming that it does.

Thank you, Rod—for what you created in our dream.
In The Twilight Zone.

By CBS Television-CBS Portrait by photographer Gabor Rona-mark is faint in spots. - eBay itemphoto frontphoto back, Public Domain, https://commons.wikimedia.org/w/index.php?curid=22101341

George Carlin

I'd like to speak with George Carlin again, please.
I am back, and I'm hearing how I gave you an outstanding chapter in The 5th Secret, *but I did not discuss my own death. I can also describe how I became God the moment I died, meaning I'm glad I died.*
How I became God has the most fascinating history, because I had never been not-God.
I pretended to be not-God, but God cannot be not-God. I am certain about it because I am God, and God has a lot of certainty about it, don't I?
How I died could not have been more incredible—and I am God, so "incredible" has to be something really incredible, I can tell you that.
What is incredible is that I survived it, meaning the death part. How I did, I'll never know—going from being a comedian in life, to becoming God in death. I never considered that I was God, or I wouldn't have been a very good comedian. God has a sense of humor— God made humans TO LAUGH AT OURSELVES!
God had a big laugh in my case, because I did not know that all my jokes were about myself!
I wish I had known, then I could have made them all God jokes, which no one would think is funny.
I could have had God in all of my jokes–then I could have the God Comedy Club, which is in a church—and

instead of having donations, I would give out a lot of healing comedic insights—in the hopes that everyone dies from healing in them. I could have a "mass funeral mass" at the same time—IT WOULD BE HILARIOUS!—everyone becoming God in a COMEDY CLUB CHURCH!... talk about having a choir of angels...

How can I help you, now that I'm dead and God?

Were you met by angels before or after you died?

I had met a lot of angels, but having died made me an angel afficionado. Did you know that a lot of angels have no wings, and can be dogs or cats, and other pets? One angel that had helped me was a canary named 'Mary'.

Mary the Canary. I asked her if her name could be more scary... I assume it was a "she" with a name like "Mary", but I can never be sure—and I don't want to know, nor do I care.

Maybe I could be "Gary, quite Contrary with the Canary Mary." It has a lot of "airy" sounds, so I could be "Gary, the quite Contrary Fairy with Canary Mary," but it might not be as convincing as just "Gary" or "George"—like I had been in life.

Now I am "God George," so I don't mind what I'm called as long as I am God. I am God, having lived and died as "George," but I healed my "Georgeness," and I am still God with a healed George aspect.

Now aspects are interesting as angel aspects are. I have a lot of aspects, I can tell you that much.

I can only heal each one, and it keeps me going infinitely. I could use a little help from my angel aspects, but they are only there to help you.
I am God having only aspects to heal. I might need an eternity for some of my aspects. If I heal all of them, I do not need infinity anymore—then how could I even exist? I could create infinite lifetimes, in infinite timelines, and then it would never end.
How could it ever end if it is a dream that never existed? It couldn't—I am God, and I am certain. I am you in my certainty, having a little uncertainty to heal.

Thank you, George—or God George—you are right.
I am God in all of my aspects becoming certain that they are not only aspects, but God having only one aspect—infinite lovingness.

Dad

Is there someone else I should include in this book, *The Moment of Death*?
Allow me an inclusion into your book, please. This is your Dad, and I had been invited into All About the Soul's Journey.

Hi, Dad!
Hello Paul, I have been admiring all of the detailed accounts in your writing, and I would like to add my account, if I may.

Yes, please.
At the moment I died, it was an exhilaration beyond any comparison, except like opening a bottle of champagne. It is an incredibly healing burst of lightness in your head—although it is not without your allowing and choosing it.
My allowing it, healed my not having to choose it. Having a healed mind means having only one choice, and it is choosing love in each moment—as you have been writing about.
Having a healed mind allows all awareness into your mind. "All awareness" means allowing God and God's angels into a lightness and lovingness that is only in God making itself one with you. "Making itself one with you" was never not one with you.
It is allowing yourself to be aware of this healing truth.

Thank you, Dad!
I am healed in the Mind of God, meaning I am one with God, lighting infinitely.

GEORGE WASHINGTON

Can I speak with President George Washington?
I am always in your guidance and support.

Are you a spirit guide?
I am always guiding all who are hearing me, and I know you can always hear me.

What would you like to tell me?
I can always guide you in your consciousness research. It allows me an opportunity to go into an awareness of how my city on the Potomac has become an abomination of all I had been advocating for. Not having indentured servitude is one good thing I can acknowledge. Everything else is an abominable destruction of peoples' personal liberties.

I know, and can list them, though the U.S. government's only job is to keep the peace.
I could give you a lot longer list having nothing to do with keeping the peace.

Can you tell me what it was like when you died? I understand that you were very sick, and doctors kept blood-letting.
I acknowledge having my blood drained was not in my best interest, and it weakened me to not allow me to fight an infection in my throat. I could have healed in having more time, but my time had come to its conclusion. I had no interest in living in that much pain.

I had a lot of helpful angels come into my room before I died, although I was mostly in a state of delirium. In a flash of light, I had gone from a dying man to a living in lightness being, having no earthly interests or pain any longer. Angels acknowledged my new healed state, and asked me if I could imagine myself meeting God—and I could not imagine it.

The angels found it amusing that I could not imagine myself meeting God, informing me that I am God, incredibly not knowing that I am. It made all in my head become a lot brighter than the incredible brightness that it was.

Then what happened?

I went away from the Earth in my incredible brightness, and have become all I can possibly be now—a guiding force for all those having an interest in listening.

What would you like to say to people now, 226 years after your death in 1799?

In my life as George Washington, the first President of the United States, I could have done more to curb the destructive growth of government. I could have made all of the member States their own branch of government funding, having no Federal funding mechanisms.

> The original federal government was funded through the Funding Act of 1790, which allowed the federal government to assume the debts incurred by the states during the Revolutionary War. This act facilitated the issuance of U.S. Treasury Securities to bondholders, thereby stabilizing the nation's finances and establishing public credit.
> W Wikipedia ⓘ treasurydirect.gov

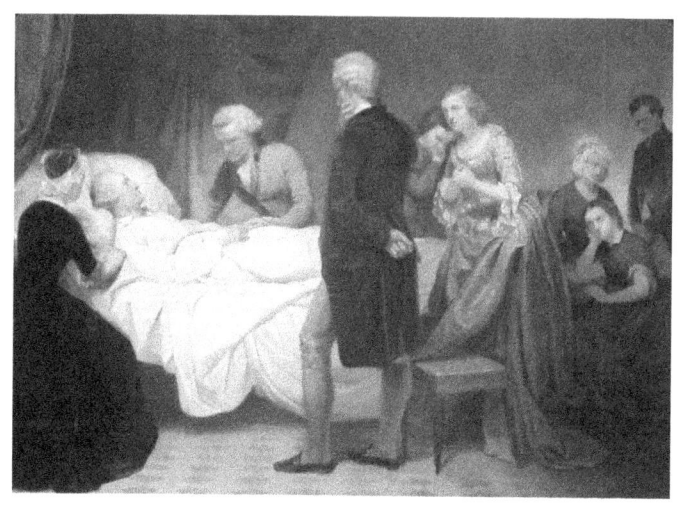

Edgar Cayce

Can you please tell me about your death experience? You had a stroke in September 1944, and died in January 1945, at age 67.
All I can hear in your mind is if I am going to give you details of my death experience.

I am a guide, having been invited into a dream you are having—that all in your lifetime is a real experience, but it is a dream of having a lifetime on Earth. How can awakening from a dream be called "death"? Here is my account of awakening into all awareness, healing, and love.

I had been always having migraine headaches, and my most debilitating one had made me partially paralyzed. I had had a stroke. This made me bedridden for the next few months, until I awakened.

In my bed, I had angels and other guides visiting me, giving me healing information for myself.

An angel had been my guardian for my entire life, although I had not consulted with it before.

I made it my final reading, you could say. I had not even considered my own health, even though I gave health advice to hundreds of others. I could have gotten a lot of health advice for myself, but I did not have that as an objective in my dream of life.

I can describe my death experience now—I know it is on your mind. I had been consulting with my guardian angel, and it was giving me a lot of healing information. It asked me if I could imagine being totally healed in the Mind of God, illuminating like an angel. I said I could not imagine being like an angel, or totally healed in the Mind of God.

In that moment, I had an incredibly intense light in my head, and I left my body and entered into the light.

I have been illuminating in it, and have been counseling others in their dream of life, and in their awakening into all awareness, healing, and love.

Thank you, Edgar. Can people call on you for healing intuitions and answers?
All I can counsel them on is allowing healing—it is always all around them.

Can you please give me one piece of advice on how to allow healing?
"I allow God in my mind, and my desire to heal becomes one with God—making it my reality. That is my daily affirmation."

Thank you again.
I am healing in the minds of all who are reading this.

BOB HOPE

Bob Hope died of pneumonia at home in 2003, at the age of 100. A few years earlier, when asked where he would like to be buried, he replied, "Surprise me."

Bob, can you please tell me about your experience when you died?
I can always have my corpse reenact it for you. I could get a lot of laughs by having myself be alive again, and to die in a more convincing way. It did not convince most people the first time.

Ha, ha!
I had a lot of people to convince—my doctor especially. He said I could continue like I was for a few more years, if I stayed in bed.

Haa, haa!
I can describe my death, but it may not be convincing. My doctor assures me that I am going to be fine.

You haven't changed.
I am an aspect of God, and God never changes—only all of its God aspects can change.

If they haven't changed, then they either are God having no need to change, or they are not improving to become like God—making a change for good. I changed in life, but mostly in death.

I should have done it sooner. I can hear in your mind—you are asking me what it was like.

I had been discussing my not-very-premature death with an angel in my bedroom, and the angel gave me a lot of instructions on how I could become a dead comedian, and asked me if I thought I could make it be funny.

I said I could laugh at my life, and if it wasn't funny, then I could die—not from laughter, but from the prospect of not being funny. After I laughed at my life, I died anyway—and I couldn't have been more relieved.

I died after laughing at my life, making the last laugh on me.

What happened next?
I had been laughing and dying, making myself the punchline, as an aspect of God.

God gave me an insight I had not considered—I was God having as many aspects to heal as I wanted.

I could have healed all of them in an instant, or in a hundred years in my case—but I didn't find healing myself to be very funny, until my last moment on the Earth. Then I became God, having nothing I could want because I was everything. I can be funny if that is my desire, but I don't need to be anything—I have to desire it.

I can desire a lot of things, but I don't need to desire anything—that is for my aspect as you to desire it, and to heal it—coming back to me in a healed state of not needing to heal.

Healing makes all God aspects one again—like a moth having just died in your cup of hot tea.

It died and allowed itself to be one with God again.

I tried to save it.
It had no need to have you save it. It could have always saved itself.

Here we consider helping or saving a life to be the highest acts of charity.
I always had my charity events, but did I save anybody? I healed them by allowing them to have humorous moments and memories.

Thank you very much, Bob—for this message with humor and insights.
I can hear you asking if I went away from the Earth. I did, and I did not. Having a place in my mind to go to is just that—in my mind. How could I go anywhere if time and space are illusions?

I am in God, which is in you, which is in God, and so on—which makes an infinite healing layering that needs to be unlayered by loving all the layers—no matter how much they need to be unlayered.

I call it, "Collapsing the layers into one layer of love— making a layer cake that healed as it collapsed."

That's a great metaphor, or analogy.

In the analogy, each layer has a need to collapse because it is not healed—and it can only be healed in your mind, believe it or not.

Wow.
Allowing it to heal, allows it to love itself and collapse.

That is a very empowering insight. Here on the Earth, we see a lot of what we wouldn't allow.
Allowing it allows it to collapse into another layer that doesn't need healing in your mind.

God exhibits itself only in your mind, which is in God, which is in your mind, and so on.

I will allow everything I see to heal in my allowing it to collapse into one layer of love.
I could call it, "A cake with one layer—a layer of collapsed needs that are no longer needed."

In the cake mix is a lot of allowing, and a cup of love—making it all stick together. Let it bake—for 100 years in my case—then put it in God Mind for eternity.

Thank you, Bob—I will.
If you don't have 100 years, it can be as long as you wish.

George Burns

Who should I speak with next about their moment of death?
All I can add is that I am healed in my mind, and in God Mind—allowing us to be one again.

George Burns here. How come I didn't have a life like Bob Hope? I could have, but I would have collapsed in all of the healing it needed—so I didn't. I wanted nothing to do with it.

Ha!
I allowed its healing to collapse itself. That's how it works here—which is neither here, nor there.

It is everywhere, which is in your mind only. How's that for a conundrum?

Thank you, George. What can you tell me about it?
All you can heal in your mind will heal in your life, if you allow it to heal. Not healing means you are not allowing it.

How can I heal all in my mind—without dying?
Allow healing by affirming, "I am God and allow everything in my mind to heal. I am God and have no need for healing—so I allow everything, and need nothing."

I don't want anything, and don't want healing— I allow it. allowing, and not wanting makes me

one with God, which I am. I am one with myself, and healing myself is unblocked.

I have one more addition to your affirmation, "I am all I can ever be, which is God myself having no illusions of not being healed."

I read that you died at home of heart failure, in 1996, at age 100. Can you please tell me what it was like?

I had a long life, and it may have been longer than necessary, but it was a really good one.

"George, how could it have been longer than necessary?" I hear in your mind.

In life, it is only necessary for love to heal you, and I had healed. I lived on for my love of life to be healing for others. I did as much as I could in the medium of radio, and then on television.

It healed many in their hearing my humorous insights. Nothing heals like humor—except dying, which can be humorous in a deadly kind of delivery.

I had been asked by an angel if I could imagine dying and being God—like in the movie 'Oh God', that I portrayed God in. I asked the angel if I could be an angel this time, and it laughed at my question.

"How come I can't be an angel?" I asked. I had been an angel in my life many times, it replied.

After I acknowledged that I could have been an angel in many instances, my head exploded in lightness and lovingness that is impossible to describe. I can always try because I am God, and can do anything now. I was God in my life, and could have done anything—but didn't realize it then.

As God, I can heal all that needs healing, I couldn't unheal it if I tried. It is a one-way healing adventure that everyone is on. Healing only has to be allowed. It can also be disallowed—it is always your choice.

"How can I always allow healing?" I hear you asking. You don't have to do anything. It is in you, and all around you. Just claim it by affirming this, "I love my healed mind, and my healed body. I am God, and all I can do is love them both. I love all they allow me to create in my life."

Hey, that's pretty good—one of the best affirmations yet.
I know. It can be our secret connection for manifesting all that your heart desires.

I really love it.
Alright, how can it not heal you if you love it? It can't. It can only heal because love is what I am.

In the beginning, you said, "...is neither here nor there. It is everywhere—which is in your mind only. How's that for a conundrum?" Can you please explain that?
Imagine having no home, and no address to go to—and being at home is always in your imagination.

If it is in your imagination, then it could be anywhere and anything you want.

If it could be anything and anywhere you want, then it must be infinite—only limited by your imagining.

'Infinite' means 'in-finite' which is defined, but God is not defined unless you assign it a definition of mostly limiting words. If you do not define God, then it is unlimited in your mind—which has only you to explore its having no limitations. If it has no limitations, that means it cannot have a time or location—both needing boundaries. If it has no boundaries, and it is in your mind—then God is having a dream of you having boundaries to heal into Oneness in each moment—not having a time, or a location.

God is in each moment of no limitation—which is in your mind.

Can it be more than an instance of lovingness in your mind? No, because lovingness is unlimited—everything else is limited by your mind.

"Why is only lovingness unlimited?" I hear in your mind. Because it is what God had promised you in your inception, to heal in a lifetime of limited time, and unlimited choices—with one unlimiting choice—love.

That is an awesome explanation. Thank you, George.
I am God and unlimited now, but you can call me 'George'.

Jimmy Stewart

Can I speak to Jimmy Stewart about his death?
Jimmy here—I have a lot to relate about my death experience, although I cannot be as descriptive as George Burns in my account.

First, I can tell you about your role in my having this opportunity to express it.

"Express it" means God hearing it and speaking it at the same time.

God is what hears it, and you are God having a desire to speak it—writing it, in this case.

I had a wonderful life, as one of my best-loved movies is named. Having had a wonderful life means I could not have asked God for anything more. I had all that a life on Earth could hope for—in Hollywood anyway. How could I have asked for more?

There is no more in Hollywood, except for healing instances in your mind.

How could I have healed my mind? I could have healed my mind by having only loving, peaceful, and kind thoughts. In an era of answering my calls for duty, I allowed myself instances of contributing to war efforts.

My father did also, but he chose rescue missions over bombing missions in World War II.

I agree that he made healing choices for everyone involved.

After your wife, Gloria died in 1994, you decided not to replace the battery in your pacemaker, and you died 3 years later, at the age of 89.

I did, and it healed me tremendously. I can hear you asking if I was met by an angel.

I always had conversations with my guardian angel, and discussed my death a lot in my last few months of life. I had been given assurances that I would be going back to God, and there was nothing I had to worry about. I never had a lot to worry about, but I did have concerns about dying.

I could not imagine losing my life. It had a lot of certainty, and a lot of uncertainty about it.

How could it have both? I don't know—that's what concerned me. I can tell you with certainty now that it is the most awesome, exhilarating, healing event that anyone could ever hope for.

I felt like I got blasted into the air, and I could fly or float in it. As I hovered in my advanced awareness, I was greeted by a lot of people I had known, including Gloria, my wife in that lifetime.

They all had a huge welcoming reception for me. I could not have been happier than when they said I was in eternity, and would live in it forever. They explained that I had never left, but had a dream that I did. My dream had been wonderful, but I can imagine that many lives are like a bad dream.

All of them have a healing purpose, and healing them gives each one its own meaning.

Its purpose and meaning are combined in the moment of death when a life is completed, and awakens in the Mind of God.

I would also ask God if it could become one with you in your dream, without having to die first.

God answers in the affirmative always, allowing you to allow God, and so on.

"I allow God, because how could I not if I am God?" is an affirmation that heals your mind.

Thank you, Jimmy.
I am God, allowing myself an instance of you having a dream that you are not God—but now it is impossible not to know. I healed your mind.

Leslie Nielsen

Leslie Nielsen died in his sleep from pneumonia in 2010, at the age of 84.
His grave market says, "Let 'er rip." Can I speak with Leslie about his death?

Leslie here—I'm not dead, even though I might look it. How could I be dead if I'm always around, and I am conversing with you? I am alive and unwell, meaning I'm 'dead and loving it'—as a movie I had been in was called. Not that I'm always listening in on your thoughts, but I am listening in now in my peeping mode. You have a lot I can listen in on in my spare time, peeping in timelessness. How can my peeping help you?

I heard that I can help by describing my death experience, although I'm not really dead.

Nothing is really dead, just one body less, more or less. Having one body less means allowing all earthly and ego concerns to die in an instant, having no more importance than the moment before, when they had no importance then either.

That makes me not really dead, except in an ego and earthly sense—although I can be back in, up and around if I choose to be.

What was it like when you died?

I am not as dead as I look, but I was having a discussion with an angel, when I realized where angels really are. I had a feeling I was not in Kansas anymore, Toto.

How could all I believed in be half imaginary, and half not true? I mean, how could it be half imaginary and half imagination, and still be partly true?

It can be if it has love in it, because love is what created it—for you to discover it.

Here is the catch that allows you to discover it—it has to be coming from inside of you for it to be allowed on the outside of you. It has to be that way in an illusion of light and dark, if you have the light inside of you.

Think how love could be all around you if it isn't coming from you. It only has one source in each person's universe. How could it be any other way in an imaginary illusion?

Thank you, Leslie.
I thank you, half in the illusion I am peeping into, and half in awareness in the Mind of God—where God has infinite peepers.

PART II

EXCERPTS FROM
ALL ABOUT THE SOUL'S JOURNEY

Hillen

We'll talk about that, but I'd like to start at the beginning—or what we consider the ending. What did you experience before you passed away?

I accepted ending life as I knew it, and angels came all around me in the hospital bed. I acknowledged a guardian angel that had always been near me in my life. All healed in my mind as we discussed the life I had chosen to learn from.

We had a long discussion in terms of finding healing in all of my thoughts in love, and in peace.

All of a sudden, I had a flash of light in my mind that could not be brighter, making all of my lifetime concerns evaporate in it.

Acclimating to that brightness, I was then heading into it myself—meaning I must have died at that point.

A long, illuminated hollow tube opened up in the top of my head, and I was pulled into it. After I entered it, half of my body was not going to be with me any longer, meaning my physical body. My Light Body had become my healed body.

As I left the Earth, I could see I was getting farther away from it as I headed into the Earth light ring of all consciousness.

In the Earth ring of consciousness, I could be all that God promised me at my inception—all lovingness, gentleness, and peacefulness.

Were you greeted by other beings or predeceased relatives after you died?

A lot of people I knew helped me to acclimate after I arrived in the Earth ring of consciousness.

Do you have surroundings that are like a physical place?

All I am enveloped in is loving energy that holds me in a condition of blissfulness and love for all that I can imagine.

What kind of things do you imagine?

I imagine that I am flying like a bird around the world, and everything I look at is healed in my imagining it healed.

My imagining it healed heals it in my mind, allowing my mind to heal, and so on.

Can you see angels?

Angels are everywhere and heal my thoughts if I ask them to help me—as you can do in life.

What do angels look like?

Angels look like what you might imagine, having wings and only loving intentions.

Pete

The moment you died, did you have the opportunity to go back in time 1/2 second before the death moment, to change the outcome and live?
All death is agreed upon beforehand, so the decision is made, but can be delayed if the person wants it to be— even if they have died a few seconds before that.

Can it be more than a few seconds?
Sure, as long as there is a body that can function, and a pineal gland entry point.

What did you feel after you died?
I could hear another person crying, and could see a wrecked car crashed into a pole. I didn't acknowledge that I was in the car until after an ambulance came, and I could hear my name when they were talking.

What happened next?
All I could do was hope that Mom and Dad would not be devastated, because I did not want to come back into my body and live.

Then what?
An angel came and asked me if I was alright and wanted to go ahead into an advancement of healing that was almost like being in perfect peacefulness and lovingness.

What was the angel like?

It looked like angels we imagine, but it had a long, willowing robe that illuminated, flowing all around itself.

Let's go back to where you said, "A death is agreed upon beforehand." Who agrees to it, and when?
A death is agreed upon by God and yourself, always in the last moment, but sometimes even before you are born.

Jackie

Can you please tell me what it was like to die?
A lifetime ending can be however you want it to be. In my case, it was in a hotel in Russia.

Each lifetime ending can be the most exhilarating experience, finally to be free of earthly cares that are not important.

As I died, my head illuminated intensely, and the light had a long tunnel in it. Going into it was not a choice, but rather all I could do. All healed in my mind and heart at that moment—not in my heart, but in my spirit's heart.

All death meant was healing in ecstasy in that moment—an ecstasy enveloping me in love from God in that moment.

Going into the tunnel seemed like a long time, but it was not. A long time on Earth is an instant in the spirit realm.

It all happened instantly. As I left my body, I was leaving the Earth behind—ending my life as I knew it.

Ending life can be a welcome event.

The next eventful moment was that a guide met me and asked me if I knew where I was.

Not being absolutely sure, I said "I don't know." An angel approached me and said I was in the higher realm of heaven, finding healing in my mind from all that I had experienced in my lifetime on Earth.

"Imagine an angel telling me that!" was all I could think at that moment.

Next, I was invited into a place where all of the Earth life memories are reviewed. I could hear and experience all of them—not just from my perspective, but from everyone else's perspective—and you were in many of them.

Dave & Russell

What should people expect at the moment of death?

All of their lifetime cares will disappear into a ball of light that envelopes all of their lifetime cares and disappointments, all in one healing flash of God in your mind that is so strong, it makes you feel like you are God for that moment.

After initial contact with God, they can expect to leave the planet, and accept all they had lived for and became.

Next, it will become apparent that their minds had healed in losing their egos.

All of this happens in about a second in your time, and actually it is less than a second.

After that, you are met by a guide or an angel that helps you to get oriented in the spirit world.

It understands everything about your life and your purpose. It guides you into a classroom of about 80 spirits you have known in many lifetimes, and all of them are elated to be in your presence—and "elated" here means ecstatic.

"Is anyone elated here to see me?"—I know you are thinking. Earth has its disappointments; each will heal in time, or in each person's moment of death.

Each of them has a message for you, and can't wait to share it. All of them believe in you, and in your healing objectives, because each one has helped you along the way.

David R.

1958—1999 (aged 41)
Howard County, Maryland, USA

Russell J.

1958—2018 (aged 59)
Tyler, Smith County, Texas, USA

Wayne

What was it like when you died? As you probably know, I am making a book to help people understand death.
It allowed me all the freedom in the universe, and healed me in my mind at the same time.

Please describe the process.
A higher energy came into my head, and I saw an angel that accepted all that I was, in all of my lifetimes.

It alternated in healing me, and showing me how I came into being as a human.

After I died, it illuminated my entire being, which actually was limitless.

Having no limits was absolutely exhilarating. I could envision anything, and it would become real.

What is an example?
I was a bird, flying along a coastline—actually hearing the waves and feeling the air lift me higher.

Another instance was that I could learn anything I wanted by allowing all the information into my mind.

Do you know what God is?
God is all that you are, and even more because it has no limits like you do.

Are my limits self-imposed?

Almost all of them are limits in your mind, yes—and all are eliminated at the time of death.

What happened next?

I acclimated myself to controlling my thoughts so I could heal all that I had to heal from my lifetime on Earth.

Another angel had come to help me understand what I was going into in the next moment.

I accepted its instructions, and instantly was inside of a chamber of a council meeting, I thought.

All of the council members knew all about my lifetimes. All of them had advice for me, and it was mainly healing information that I could instill into my soul.

As soon as I acknowledged all of their advices, I departed in an instant, and appeared in a classroom of other spirits I have known for all of my entries into lifetimes.

BUCK

Can you tell me what it was like when you died?
I actually have no memory of it because I was asleep, but my energy body had become free of all cares it once had.

When did you realize you had died?
After the first moment of being in a carefree energy form.

What happened next?
I came into a lightness that cannot be described in words. An angel came closer to me and asked me all about my illness, and it told me what had happened. After I accepted all it had explained, I followed its instructions to go into the lightness further.

After I entered into even more lightness, all I could feel was God loving me unconditionally.

All I wanted was to stay in that feeling forever, and allow it to heal me forever.

Weren't you healed instantly?
I was healed in my energy body, but my soul needed more help from God.

What happened after that?
I and God became one for a moment of acceptance, and that instant recognition made my soul heal immensely—not that unlimited can be "immensely."

After I healed immensely in my soul, my angel came and accompanied me to a classroom where a lot of souls were, and all of them acknowledged me in the most loving and accepting way that healed me more.

I acknowledged all of them, and it healed all of them also—in the heart of their energy bodies.

Marty

Would you like to tell me what death is like?
It allows me ecstasy, freedom, healing, and knowing—all in blissfulness, wrapped in lovingness from God.

What happened right before you died?
An angel had come to check on me, and we talked for longer than I had realized. It made me feel okay with any decision to live, or not to live. I decided to continue on my journey, since living would not be advantageous for my soul.

What happened next?
After the angel had gone, I was happy with my decision, and I died a little while later after God also came into my mind, because I was asking God for help.

Imagine a light in your head so strong, it makes you illuminate also. It held me in it, and there was a hole in it that I got pulled into.

Next, I left the Earth, and got further and further away until I came to a place where it was all lightness.

Getting there was the easy part. Now I had to heal myself. I entered a large room like a theater, and the film was my life—from my perspective, and also from other peoples' perspectives. How I made them feel was the plot of the film.

Mostly, I did not do that much damage. I damaged myself by holding onto earthly things that I no longer had a use for.

That includes mental items also. Anyhow, I healed in losing my life, instead of my things.

Life allows us to heal in each moment by deciding what we do not want, versus what we do want.

Allow what you do want by not hating what you do not want—just let it go.

I never knew you to hate anything.
I hated all of the injustice in the world. Allow it to heal itself—it cannot heal by hating it.

Lynda

Why did you leave here at such a young age?
I was an artist, and the Earth to me was not very beautiful. Now, I can only feel love, and I only see beauty.

I am really glad to hear from you.
Beauty becomes all that you see if you look for it. Hating all that is not beautiful only creates more for your hating to see.

Would you like me to include your death, or after-death experience?
Absolutely—it was magnificent! I healed instantly in my mind, allowing beauty in, in infinite degrees of beautification—actually, allowing God healing love in is the best description.

What else can you tell me about it?
All beauty came into my head, and all non-beauty left it. I ceased being Lynda, and became all that God intended me to be—allowing all that had been me to heal instantly. All I could ever imagine was instantly in my presence, so I had to focus on healing and beauty.

After all I had imagined as beauty was in my presence—actually in and as my presence—it actually was my presence in all the beauty I could imagine, I allowed myself and God to be in Oneness.

It sounds perfect.
It is perfect, making all of life a perfect dream to heal ourselves in.

Rich

Can you tell me what it was like when you died?
It was actually a gift from God in that moment, allowing all that was unwell in my life to disappear.

Then what happened?
I accepted my fate, meaning that I would die from cancer—not an aggressive cancer, but an aggressive cancer treatment.

Were you visited by an angel?
Actually, I was, and it made me feel good about my fate.

Please continue.
I could have continued my life, but it was not in my best interest from my soul's perspective.

All I could do was heal myself in those final moments until a light came into my head that was unbelievably intense, but it was good for my healing though. It healed my mind, and my body detached from it, making everything about me only lightness.

Initially, I thought that was all there is, but I had more to heal. All of a sudden, I was getting higher and higher above the Earth, and I could feel only lovingness in everything I could hear and see from there.

Hearing all of the sounds of nature and of life was the most interesting. I had not heard it all at once like that.

Hearing it all at once made me feel alive, and healed.

Following my course higher made me notice that feelings I had not healed started entering into my mind—all interrupting my loving, healed state of mind. Finally, they healed as I allowed them to heal.

I could detail them, but you can imagine how many, and what kinds of thoughts they were.

After I acclimated to having only loving thoughts, a guardian angel came and said it would guide me into my classroom where everything is explained, and we are all tested to make sure we understand.

Did you have a Lifetime Review?

Actually, I had a Lifetime Review when I was in the hospital, going in and out of consciousness.

All I could do was heal my thoughts, and hope they stayed healed after that.

Loriann

Can you tell me what dying was like?
I remember a crashing sound like a car wreck, but I was not in the car. I was above it and looking down at it. I imagined that it could have been a bad accident, and did not know that I was in the car.

Do you think that your spirit left your body right before the crash?
It did—I'm a chicken for that kind of trauma.

So, it was definitely painless.
Not only painless, it was wonderfully invigorating ecstasy!

Did you stay at the accident scene?
I heard an ambulance, and then I left the area.

Did you know that you had died in the crash?
No, I was feeling as good as ever.

When did you realize it?
After I heard my family crying about me.

Your kids?
And my husband, and all of my family.

Where did you go when you left the accident scene?
After I had been around my family members, hoping they could hear that I'm not really dead—I accepted

the already obvious conclusion that they cannot hear me.

An angel came and held my hand, and told me it was a necessary and healing event for all of them.

After I accepted that, it gave me instructions on what we were going to do next—meaning, after I could get the courage to leave the planet.

Get ready for this part because it is amazing! All I could feel was God loving me in the most fantastic, complete, and intense way that I didn't want anything else. I ascended higher and higher until I was away from the Earth.

I made it to heaven! Another angel came toward me and guided me higher into an incredible lightness.

After I arrived in the higher lightness, I came into a large room that had all of the spirits I know in it—having all been notified that I was coming. They gave me an incredible homecoming reception.

Was there a period of Lifetime Review?
Actually, it came after my homecoming reception. The angel accompanied me to a theater, which was another auditorium-like space. A film had been playing for me to hear and see- not only to hear and see, but to actually be in it again!—and hearing myself from other peoples' perspectives.

It could have been worse, but I know how they felt.

LORIANN
EXCERPT FROM *THE 5TH SECRET*.

I can answer your question now about how suicide will affect a person's spirit.
It can only contribute to a person's healing and learning in their lifetime, and its ending before it is completed. Healing and learning are the objectives in all lifetimes, although healing is the most important in the moment of death.

My understanding is that suicide is not natural, and the person is avoiding the lifetime challenges that they had chosen to experience, before incarnating.

It can be considered a healing and learning experience that is natural, because it was decided, and action taken to implement the idea. Not having acted in that moment would also be a natural progression in consciousness.

Good points, but will the person's spirit have to repeat the challenge that they couldn't overcome in their lifetime?

A challenge can heal in the moment of death, and it can heal in another lifetime if the person chooses it for their healing objectives.

PART III

EXCERPTS FROM
THE 5ᵀᴴ SECRET

John Candy

Can you please tell me what dying was like?
All healing, all knowing, all exhilaration, and all ecstasy in having God's love incredibly illuminate your mind.

Did an angel visit you before you died?
"Am I dead?" is what I said to the angel because I was asleep. All I could feel was an incredible light in my mind. The angel asked me if I was ready to go with it to another place that all comedic actors go to.
I followed and asked if it was a clown world where I was not allowed a costume.
It said that I would see, and could decide if I needed one. After that, I said I needed one.
It gave me one with an orange wig and a red nose, and said, "Let's go meet God."

Haaa, haaa, haaa!
It gets better because God had on the same costume that I did, and we were identical.
At that moment, I realized I was God having a dream.

Then what happened?
I had an introspection period where I reviewed my life as a clown, having a dream to clown around in. It could have been better, and it could have been worse, but I did okay—but didn't love myself as much as I could have.

Bob Newhart

What was it like to die?
It allowed me to feel how all of the books said I would feel.
An incredible brightness exploded in my head and held me in it until I started moving out of my body. All I could feel was exhilaration.
After I left my body, an angelic being and another being that had been my guide on Earth, he said, guided me higher in consciousness, and away from the Earth.
All I could feel was healed in an indescribable and all-encompassing lovingness.

Freddie Mercury

Can you tell me what it was like when you died?

All I could hear was God in my mind asking if I could come hear myself sing for it. I said, "Yes," and instantly I became what higher beings call "illuminated in God."

It healed me totally, and all I could do was have one less thing to heal—and that was my body.

I no longer had a body, and was a light being. It was magnificent, I can assure you.

An angel and a guide came to meet me, saying I was expected. After I realized I was dead, I asked both of them where we would be going. They acknowledged and answered, "We are going to God."

I acknowledged and asked, "How can we get to where God is?"

They both laughed at my question and said that I am God.

I could hardly believe it, and thought I must be having a dream. They heard my thought and said that I had just awakened from my dream.

All of a sudden, I appeared in an auditorium that had a film playing of my life. I could hear and feel everything from each person's perspective. It was an awful performance, but I had to hear and feel all of my hurtful and unloving episodes.

After all of that played, I arrived in a classroom devoid of students, and only I was in it.
I could hear myself asking what I had to do, and that is when my assignments appeared on the blackboard. It looks like I could be in eternity.

David Bowie

Were you visited by an angel before you died?
I had allowed cancer and its treatment to kill me because I needed an ending of my life to be in that window of time. An angel did come and have a conversation with me near the end, in my bedroom.
It accepted me for all that I had ever done, in all of my lifetime constructions.
After it left, an illumination in my head was so intense—actually, it was the most intense light I could ever imagine—and it was pulling me into it from my head.
I could not have been more amazed than when I left my body. I became a being healed in the light of God, meaning I was God's healed illumination of itself. A death heals into the light of God.
After I acknowledged that I was healed, I allowed my thoughts to be on healed constructions—all healed in the Mind of God, which allowed me to be one with God. Making all healed constructions was like being God.

How did you feel at that point?
I felt absolutely magnificent and enlightened. "Enlightened" has a meaning that cannot be described.
It cannot be described because a healed mind does not need anything, or a need to describe it.

At that healed point in my mind, I had a period of introspection that had all of my earthly actions illuminated on a screen that had me in each other person's position, hearing all that I was having them to hear.
I could feel all that they felt, and acknowledged that I could have been more loving.
Acknowledging that gave me a clearer picture of life from the soul's perspective.

What happened after that?
I actually had no other activities since then.

GEORGE HARRISON

Can you please tell me what the dying process was like?

An angel came into the corner of my room, and acclimated to my mind so we could talk.
I asked it many detailed questions about God and the afterlife.
It asked me if I could imagine being God, and I said I could not. It was like lightning hitting me in the head, and I couldn't believe it because God and I became one. I can't describe it fully, but I was enlightened.
All I could hear, feel, and see was love in all of creation.
Another angel came and asked me if I wanted to go into higher consciousness, and I asked, "How can there be higher than this?" It answered me in a gesture of knowing I could follow it, and I did—and both angels and I went higher and away from the Earth.
All I can do now is guide others who need guidance.

John Lennon

You were good at shocking everyone.
I always had an edginess to my creativity, and death can be a creative ending to a creative lifetime.

Did you feel pain when you were shot?
I had an initial painful sting, and allowed it to shut off in that moment. I died pretty quickly, you know.
All I could feel then was a light in my head, as if my head had exploded in that moment also.
I expected that I would get up, and I did, but my body was still on the ground.
I felt fantastic, but I could hear people yelling and making a big fuss.

What are you doing?
I am always healing in one way or another by learning how God can only be love.
Love heals in each moment, which is only in your mind.

Dr. Martin Luther King, Jr.

Can you please tell me about your death? Was your lifespan predetermined?
It had a beginning and an ending that could be altered, but I chose not to, with a reason.
Allowing myself an exit at that time was the most advantageous for my soul.
It had an impactful ending that I could have delayed or altered. I chose it in the last few months of my life. All I could do was delay it a month or more, but it concluded in the same manner.

Can you tell me what happened after you were shot?
I heard a shot in the distance, but it took me a second to realize I was hit. It felt like I got hit in the face with a bat. I lost consciousness, and have no recollections after that.
All I could feel was electrifying, delightful energy that held me in loving oneness with it.
An angel came and asked me if I could accept that I had died, and I said, "Yes."
After that, we headed away from the Earth, as I always expected I would if I was dead.

What happened after you headed away from the Earth?
A guide came and asked me if I had any questions about where I was.

"I had died," I said, "and I must be in an afterlife."
It acknowledged my answer, and asked me another question. "Has my life been a good one?" it asked.
I said, "It had a lot of difficulty, but it was good."
I then appeared in a large theater with my life having been playing in 3 dimensions on a big screen—and I alternated in each person's position to hear and feel as they heard and felt.
I could have been a lot better in many instances.

Wolfgang Mozart

Did you die from G.I. distress?
I did, and it couldn't have been soon enough.

Did you think someone was trying to kill you?
I did, although it was an imagined fear.

Can you tell me what it was like when you died?
I already stated that it couldn't have been soon enough. Angels came into my mind and told me we were going to God's house next—and a light flashed in my head so intensely that it altered my mind in a fantastic way, not having earthly pain. After I noticed its intensity, I started moving into it, although I had been enveloped in it already.
All I could feel was enlightenment, and that we had begun moving away from the Earth.
I couldn't help feeling that I had not only died, but I hadn't really lived.
I liked it in my netherworld of life and death. All I could hope for was illuminating in the Mind of God, and healing me at the same moment.
A large concert hall had enveloped me as a spectator, and all I could discern was my own life playing on the stage.
All of the parts had me in them, and I could hear and feel all of the instances how I made people feel.

After that, I continued in my netherworld, and an angel had come to accompany me in my alternate life having no more pain.

Where did you go?
We came to a school-like setting where I could learn more about my Earth life, allowing all I learned to heal me even more.

Vincent Van Gogh

Can you tell me what it was like when you died?
I had a multitude of feelings I had not felt before. I was ecstatic and free.
An angel came and informed me that I cannot die by killing myself, and allowed me to go back and live—to the time before I decided to kill myself.
I answered that I had no interest in living anymore, and it asked me, "Why not?"
I asked it, "Why?"
It explained to me about my agreement to live for about 18 more years.
I asked it in my most artistic way, "Why?" again.
It accepted my non-acceptance, and we headed higher and away from the Earth.

Then what happened?
I allowed myself an introspection period, and I acclimated myself to a new, higher existence.

Vincent van Gogh - Google Arts & Culture — mwF3N6F_RfJ4_w, Public Domain, https://commons.wikimedia.org/w/index.php?curid=21977797

BJ

Let's talk about when you did die. I saw you when you were in the hospital. You were in a coma for about a week after a piece of arterial plaque had broken off and stopped your heart.
I had a heart attack allowing my life to end in a healing event that cannot be described.
All I felt was ecstasy and expansiveness, having no earthly concerns other than my family.
I have always guided each of them with healing instructions. I call all of them, and hear all their loving thoughts about me.

Where was your spirit when your body was in a coma?
I came into the hospital all of the times your family and mine were visiting, and was in the room with everyone.

What were you thinking?
I had a lot of love for everyone, and I whispered in each person's ear that I love them, and will see them again.

Did anyone sense it?
All of them heard me in their minds, but sometimes it was registered later.

Did an angel visit you?

I was accompanied by an angel to a lightness that was incredibly intense, and it enveloped me completely.

Is that when you died, and when was it?
I had died in the first few minutes after having the heart attack, although my body had a little bit of life left.

Did you leave the Earth with the angel, and then have a Life Review?
I did. It allowed me one more opportunity to return to my body and live, but I decided I might not get as good an opportunity in the future for leaving.

Baron B.

Before you died, did an angel visit you?
I had a few angelic visitations which healed me within my heart and mind. All had my highest interest as their work to heal me.

What happened when you died?
I accepted their delicate suggestion for me to advance into higher consciousness with them, and I left in a flash of light that was incredibly intense—but it also felt incredibly good. I could hear all of the angels' words in my mind after that. Each of them had on a flowing robe that illuminated also.

Did they have a gender or race?
All of them had a beautiful appearance without a gender or racial identity.

Dave C.

Can you please tell me about the moment you died?
A light in my head alarmed me because it was so intensely bright, and I had fallen down, I remember.
Not having any mobility also alarmed me. A light being had appeared in my head and informed me that I was alright.
Hearing that made me not be alarmed anymore. Actually, I felt fine.

What happened next?
The light in my head opened, and I entered into it completely—meaning all except my physical body which had died.
After I entered the light, I went away from the world to a lightness, heavenly place.

An angel then asked me if I was okay with my decision to leave the Earth. I had an option in my decision process where I could go back to the Earth. I decided to continue with my healing in the lightness, allowing me a larger healing perspective.

Paul P.

Did angels visit you before you died?
Angels and another guide checked on me in my hospital bed about every day, asking if I could be accustomed to having a healed body.

I said, "I could" despite not knowing what it meant. At the last visit I said, "I wish I could have it," and all of a sudden, a light in my head had indescribably healed all in my mind, and in my body—meaning in my Light Mind, and my Light Body.

My already dead physical body was not going to heal the way it needed to. All I could feel was ecstasy and exhilaration, and a love having no expression that I can describe. I had died, but I am not dead.

I am alive in a world of lightness where I had an introspection that allowed me to hear and feel all I had made others feel and hear.

I had a lot of hearing and feeling to heal by loving myself. All healing is in the mind, so heal in life by loving and forgiving yourself.

Allow it to heal in your mind, and it heals your body as God's light healing in you.

Colin M.

How did you happen to die when you did? Tammy said that you lived apart, went home after an argument, and your body was found a couple of weeks later.
All I had come to accomplish in life had been accomplished, so I could leave anytime. I chose a moment when nobody was around in my home to make an exit where I could not be held back. I could have allowed myself another month or more, but had an exit opportunity in the moment I had left.

Why was it an opportunity?
I was hearing an angel in my head instilling all lovingness, and all peacefulness. With its guidance, I decided to leave my body behind.

Did you know it was an angel guiding you before you died?
I did. It explained how it had chosen me to be my guardian in life, and it guided me away from the Earth after I had died.

Was your lifespan predetermined?
It had a beginning date and an ending date, but I could have changed the ending date.

A medical intervention or a checkup would not have extended your life, correct?
I could have lived another month or so, but it was my time to leave the planet.

Doc

You are missed, Doc.
I am healing in godly light now, and it has me illuminating in it—I mean, I am lightness now. I love having healed myself, and not be a burden on my family any longer.

I'm sure they didn't feel burdened by taking care of you.
I had become incapacitated, immobile, and as unalive as you can get without being dead. My next best and biggest healing event was death.

Did an angel come visit you before you died?
I had all of my brothers and sisters who died, and my daughter had come into my head numerous times. How did all of them have knowledge of my coming departure from the Earth? I had informed all of them in our soul group that I was coming in the next 2 weeks, and they helped me heal all I could heal in my mind before leaving the Earth.

One of my favorite books is *Into the Light* by a hospice doctor, Dr. John Lerma. He said they often knew when someone was going to die because they would have visitations two weeks before, by angels and predeceased relatives— usually appearing to them up in the corner of the room.
I heard about it in my practice also.

Mack

Did you feel pain when you died?
I felt all I always believed I could feel—ecstatic lovingness, all wrapped in a peacefulness that I cannot even describe.

Did an angel or a guide meet you?
I was feeling like I was in heaven until an angel came and asked me if I was alright. Alright? I am more than alright; I am ecstatic!
It acknowledged my response, and asked me if I could imagine being back in my body again.
I said, "Why would I want to be back there again?" All of a sudden, I had the most incredibly intense light explosion in my head, and the angel and I left the Earth, as I knew it.

Then what happened?
I accepted my completely misguided attempt at not failing by failing, and I acknowledged that I could have another chance, although I did not allow myself another failure excuse to heal myself in.

You then had a period of introspection, correct?
I did, and I hurt so many people for so long, that I am in need of healing forgiveness from myself—and all of them also.

Andrew & Jay

I'd like to ask you about your brother, Jay, who was about 2 years younger than you. He died about 10 years ago, from an overdose of painkillers. He had a lot of pain in one or both of his legs from loss of circulation, then surgery, etc.

I had always advised him in his life, and he did not listen to me. He had been taking illicit drugs before losing consciousness for so long, it made his legs atrophy.

"I am here, and hear all I am allowed to hear in your conversation. I am Allison's brother Jay, and hear Allison and my mother also, in their silent wonderings. How did I die? I had an angel giving me 3 options. A first, incredibly difficult option would be to have a lifetime incapacitated from my destructive behavior.

Another option was to have my life continue as it was, without being incapacitated. I did not love it enough to continue it.

A third option was to continue on in my healed Light Mind and body, where God would meet with me. I liked that as an option, having no interest in the other two.

As I considered it, an intense light exploded in my head, and I headed into it, feeling incredibly good as I left my body.

I had died, and I loved it—although I had to live it again from everyone else's vantage point. I could hear and feel all the pain I caused my family and others. I am almost impossibly sorry for how I hurt them."

A Soul Director
Tom L.

Did an angel meet you when you died?
I was met by many angels, having heard I was coming.

Wow—what an honor!
Angels had heard I was coming because I am one who directs angels in their activities.

Aren't angels directed by archangels?
I can direct archangels and angels in my capacity as a soul director.

What is "a soul director"?
A soul director can direct all archangels, angels, and souls of people that have a need for some direction in life—meaning in their activities in life, and healing people.

Please give me an example.
I have directed angels to heal in life where they had not been asked by a person. I have directed peoples' souls to heal in life by deciding on a new line of work, or health regimen. I have more examples, but you get the idea.

Leroy

How did it go?
Angels came all around me, and one held me in its wings. We headed higher and higher away from the Earth.
I cannot describe how good I felt, and still do.
As I got higher in consciousness, I met God. God had this to say to heal me—"We are One and only One. I cannot be One without you."
"Cannot be One" means God has a limitation, and that is all I needed for my mind to heal in removing its limitation—not God's limitation, my limitation.

Wow—that is very profound. I am very happy for you, Leroy.
I am God, and had a dream of being Leroy—in a time and place that I could only imagine in a dream.

That's even more profound.
I am also God having a dream that I am you—and you are communicating with me, because it is clearly not possible for anything that is loving to be apart from God. All appearing to be apart from God is an illusion. Affirm, "I am, and you are. I am God, and God has your illusions to heal in. God doesn't need healing, only you do because healing makes light in your eternal soul, which illuminates infinitely."

Why do I need to do that?
So God can express itself in all that is good.

JOHN S.

Hi John, I was thinking about you.
I am glad you can hear in your mind, what I have in my mind. How am I now, you are wondering?
I am as good as ever, now that I am healed in an incredible lightness, having no description in words.

I remember right after you died 20 years ago, that your messages to me were pretty angry, calling your 3 cancer doctors "murderers."
At that moment, I had not been instructed how I manifested my own agreement for leaving the planet, and my earthly life.

I assume that you were met by angels and guides, given a Life Review, and have been studying your life lessons in classrooms.
I have experienced all of them in my afterlife, meaning in a lightness world I have come into.

How are you?
I am all God has promised I could be, and I do not have a need for anything else, other than a last request from you.

CHRIS T.

I expected that you would be treated and released, but you died only a day or two later.
Actually, it was after 3 more days, and I did die—having no more earthly obligations to complete.

Can you tell me what happened?
All of my obligations had been only to myself—not to anyone else, except God, which is myself.
All had been completed in that lifetime, and I could hear myself saying that it was time to go home.
In the hospital, an angel came to discuss that with me. It made me want to go with it, when I learned where we were going.
After I had accepted all it had discussed with me, an illumination in my head exploded in the most intense lightness—and all I could feel was God's love all around me and through me, healing my lifetime concerns.
A gentle pulling had me moving into the light, and out of my body through the top of my head.
I had not been more elated in my life when I was out of my body. Not having a body meant not having an ego identity anymore. I had been healed by God, not by the doctors.

Where did the angel take you?
I accepted its invitation to follow it higher and away from the Earth. I then came into a large auditorium

which had a 3-dimensional movie of my life playing on a 3-dimensional screen.

I could hear and feel what everyone else in the movie heard and felt from interacting with me.

What should I and readers of this book do, or understand while we are alive?
Act like it doesn't matter what goes on in the world, because when you're dead, it doesn't.
It only matters how it affects your ability to respond with love.

That is a very profound and important statement.
It can help you to heal what you have in your mind, not having more things to heal piled on top of it.

Marty (again)

I would really like to know what it is like in the spirit world.
It is all that I heard it is like. I am not living in time anymore, only in an instant moment.
How can 'all that is' have a time limit? It can't. Only in your mind you can limit its love for life, including itself.

[I listed my thoughts...]
And you are enveloped in love from the moment you decide your life is ending. How can it be described better?
It is like being in a heated bathtub where you are floating in warm water. In the heat is love, and the water has no limits.
It is the greatest feeling! You would love it—no pun intended. I can also describe how it will heal you.
Imagine looking into the water, and there is only the most beautiful blue light you have ever seen.
In the light is God, and God will give you anything you can think of. This is where it can be very healing, and also incredible in how tricky it is to control your thoughts.

Tell me about it—I'm all ears.
I can only give you my perspective, and other people must have a similar experience.

I imagined that I had a bird's body, and in my bird-like state, I was flying along a coastline of cliffs—on a beautiful green coastline that looked like Ireland. Having said that, I could have been anywhere that it was green and had cliffs along the coast.

In my imagining that I had flying ability, I went along the coast looking for anything that I could heal myself with.

Having especially keen eyesight gave me instance after instance of healing items that I spotted.

As I spotted them, I imagined that I was healed by them. I coasted along the coast—again, no pun intended.

Having all I could heal in my mind in that excursion, I imagined that I could be a lion that never had anything to fear.

How could I have nothing to fear? By imagining that my life was only a dream—where I was dreaming it, and it had nothing to fear in it.

Having nothing in my dream life to fear meant that I had nothing in my life but loving it.

So, you healed in your mind by exploring or experiencing what was not easily possible when you were alive?

Yes, but it is possible because it is all that I could have been in life. I could have altered my mind to be a fearless lion, or a flying bird that heals itself in all it sees.

PART IV

OTHER EXCERPTS

More Time, Or Not[1]

One thing I would like to convey to people is that when a person dies, it has been agreed to by them on both a mental level, and on a spiritual level.
They can even opt out of dying by skipping back in time to before the death moment, and live.
That is correct. Each person's death moment has to be agreed upon, and accepted by them.

When is it agreed upon, and with whom do we agree?
All agreements obligate one party only to itself, because all are one.
It is agreed upon before birth in most cases, and can also be changed by each individual in their lives having a need for more time, or not.

People who have died tell me that it is exhilarating ecstasy for them.
It acclimates a life-mind to God Mind, which can be an intensely wonderful awareness that you are not having a dream, but had just awakened from one.

What else would you like to share with me here?

---

[1] Excerpt from *The 5th Secret*.

All a death moment really is can be described as an awakening into all healing, all love, and all awareness.

How could it be agreed upon if it was not all God had promised in your agreement?

Really good point.

You can heal yourself in life by having this affirmation in your mind, "I am God and have no need for life or death, except for my godliness and lovingness to express itself in."

Angel Death[2]

Is there an angel of death?
I am the Angel of Death, as you call it—although death is an illusion.

Is death an illusion, or is the dream of life an illusion?
All dreams are illusions, making all waking up in them 'having no illusions'.
Death is having no more illusions, or not having to be in the dream anymore—meaning all death can ever be is an illusion also.

What is your name?
I am Angel Death, although having that name is a misnomer—I am alive, not having experienced death.

What do you want to tell me about death?
It is a welcome event, I can assure you. No one has been dissatisfied yet, except for those who don't know they are dead.

All who have died were alive at one time, believing they were, (a) not going to die in their lifetime, if that makes any sense, or (b) living until they die, which has to make sense—although it will be a death that leaves them with no illusions in either case.

---

[2] Excerpt from *The 5th Secret*.

The 5 Stages of Death[3]

Are there stages of a natural death?
All stages of death allow God Mind into the life-mind's illusion.

There are 5 stages in losing the illusion of life:
1. *Illumination of the life-mind illusion's impermanent existence.*
2. *Illumination of the life-mind's healing into the Light Mind with angelic visitations.*
3. *Illumination of the Light Mind of Godness, or imagining a tunnel that is being traversed.*
4. *Halting non-loving thoughts, illuminating in Oneness.*
5. *Halting all thoughts, illuminating as Oneness.*

Does Stage 4 have phases such as a Life Review, and a Next Life Preview?
All stages have illumination, allowing healing of the life-mind's illusory existence.
Halting non-love in the illusion heals it instantly.
All healing illuminations in the life-mind alternate in lifetimes in the past, and in your future—allowed in a progression in time. All of the illusory lifetimes are healing, meaning imagined in the hologram of life—

---
[3] Excerpt from *The 4 Secrets of the Universe*.

alternating its healing illumination to God Mind, perpetuating infinity.

A healing and introspective instance illuminates in the 4th stage—meaning illumination of the life-mind's non-loving thoughts or actions heal in their illumination.

Other instances in the 4th Stage illuminate highly advantageous lifetime opportunities for the life-mind to heal in.

I understand that after death we are greeted by deceased loved ones and pets.
A healing illumination in the 4th Stage is reuniting with your soul groups.

What are "*soul groups*"?
All souls are illuminating in their chosen groups— alternating healing in them, and healing in God Mind. All are likened to a school's clubs and grade levels.

What other features are there in the dying process?
A loving angel guides each soul to its home in God Mind—healing, illuminating, and facilitating its journey into the light.
Angelic healing allows the life-mind to illuminate in God Mind, healing into Oneness.

After a person dies, how long does it take to have their Life Review in the timeline on Earth?
A finished lifetime review in the 4th Stage of dying takes an instant in the Mind of God—about an hour in the life-mind's timeline.

Does the person's spirit leave the scene of death then?

A healing angel's guidance halts non-love in the mind of each one it accompanies, meaning it depends how long it takes for the life-mind to heal itself.

What is an average length of time for a life-mind to heal itself?

About an hour and a half for most people.

What does a person's spirit feel at that point?

All holistic, immeasurable lovingness, peacefulness, and illumination in Oneness. Halting non-love illuminates in ecstasy.

A Guardian Angel[4]

What happens next after death?
Your lifetime review holds open one more opportunity for the spirit to return to the half second before the death moment, and live.

Dodge that bullet, so to speak,
Altering the outcome in time, yes.

Many who have had Near Death Experiences said that they were met by a guide or a light being that gave them instructions or guidance. What is that?
All will meet their guardian angel after leaving the body in dealing in death.

Does everyone have a "*guardian angel*"?
All people have an angel, animals have nature spirits, all plants have internal spirits, all minerals have mineral spirits, and all micro-organisms have an upper and lower spirit, depending on the lifetime function of the organism.

Please tell me about guardian angels.
A loving angel is assigned to each person in the lowering through the birth canal.

And the angel will help us throughout our lives as long as we ask, and then listen?

---

[4] Excerpt from *The 4 Secrets of the Universe.*

Listen, and then heed the angel's guidance.

Besides having a guardian angel, do we also have spirit guides?
Almost always, yes.

Spirit guides have lived on Earth before, but angels have not?
Not necessarily in the past; they could have lived in the present definition of 'future'.

Once you had said that we are like deep-sea divers looking for pearls of wisdom, and our guides are on the boat. What is the boat?
A loving, lifetime healing vessel.

What is the air hose?
Loving life support.

What is the ocean?
An ocean healing in the life-mind likens to Oneness healing twoness in a life-mind impermanent suit.

What is the diving suit?
The life-mind's separation in an ocean of Oneness, all motioning in the life-mind's perception of separation.

What is the shore?
All of the life-mind's fears or limitations.

What are the sought after pearls?
Nothing that the life-mind doesn't already possess. Loving life in the life-mind is the lifetime pearl, meaning the treasure promised on the boat of healing.

What would be the boat's name?
'Lifetime Healing [insert your name]'.

A Person's Spirit[5]

Do recently deceased loved ones send us signs that they are okay?
After my father died, we were writing his Eulogy in the dining room, and the chandelier kept turning off and on rapidly. When I returned to my office building at 11 PM that night, a cardinal bird started tapping on my window. It was pitch black outside because the security light was off, and birds don't fly at night.
Almost feeling like they are in the room without a body, a person's spirit can activate lighting, or animate a bird's behavior.

Could a spirit move furnishings?
A light object such as a book or paper.

Can a spirit animate other creatures besides birds?
A bird has flying ability, making it more aligned with a person's spirit.

Speaking of animals, you said that deceased pets will greet us when we die, as well as pre-deceased loved ones. Is that correct?
All that you love halts non-love in your thinking of them. Halting non-love opens your life-mind to God

---
[5] Excerpt from *The 4 Secrets of the Universe*.

Mind, meaning all healed in Oneness. Pets and loved ones illuminating in Oneness heal your life-mind by illuminating in it, meaning illuminating healing in it. All heal into Oneness in the half-second after death.

Do they really meet us, or is it our imagining?
All in Oneness is not imagined, only real.

Are deceased pets and relatives still individual souls when in Oneness?
All heal the illusion of separation in life, and in their soul illuminating individuations.

So, when we die, our life-minds heal, but our spirits continue to heal?
After death, a life-mind no longer exists, and a spirit individuation continues on its journey of infinite healing.

Afterword
Cleopatra

What did you look like as Cleopatra in your lifetime? I understand you were also known for your beauty.
I always had my hair in a long 'hairport', as it had been called then.

It is called 'braided', or 'wound into a twisted rope' now.

I had a lot of hair in my last days, as it was never cut shorter.

I had my black hair oiled, and it made it shiny black.

I had medium to light-browned skin, and I always covered most of it, in my culture. I had a medium build, and was not considered as large as would be most desirable in my lifetime.

I could be considered as having a pretty face and appearance.

Does the computer image I'm looking at right now resemble you at all?
It does in many respects, but not my hair. I had a lot of hair, and it had to be rolled up into a hairport kind of headdress.

I can look at another picture if you have one.

Did you wear tunic-type gowns?
All I had could be described as half-gown, and half-tunic- having no openings for my skin to be seen.

I can hear you asking about my favorite, or most used colors.

I liked gold, with a little green in the designs that had been embroidered.

I'll scroll through some pictures, and you tell me if there is a strong Cleopatra resemblance.

I can add my comment to the nearest resembling picture.

I found this assortment of images.

I looked a lot like all of them, except my arms were always covered.

Image courtesy of OpenArt.AI

Affirmations

"I allow all of the other people in my dream to be all I am not willing to be—unhealed egos in self-hating egoland, not having any gratitude or love for its ego demands." (pg. 23)

"I allow God in my mind, and my desire to heal becomes one with God—making it my reality. That is my daily affirmation." (pg. 52)

"I am God and allow everything in my mind to heal. I am God and have no need for healing—so I allow everything, and need nothing." (pg. 58)

"I am all I can ever be, which is God myself having no illusions of not being healed." (pg. 59)

"I love my healed mind, and my healed body. I am God, and all I can do is love them both. I love all they allow me to create in my life." (pg. 60)

"I allow God, because how could I not if I am God?" (pg. 65)

"I am, and you are. I am God, and God has your illusions to heal in. God doesn't need healing, only you do because healing makes light in your eternal soul, which illuminates infinitely." (pg. 120)

"I am God and have no need for life or death, except for my godliness and lovingness to express itself in." (pg. 130)

"Each soul in entering the material experience does so for those purposes of advancement towards that awareness of being fully conscious of the oneness with the Creative Forces."

—Edgar Cayce

About the Author

From God Mind:

*Paul Gorman illuminates as a spiritual researcher,
writing his discoveries into books,
allowing healing in the minds
of all who read them.*